Greater Than a Tourist Book
Series
Reviews from Readers

I think the series is wonderful and beneficial for tourists to get information before visiting the city.

-Seckin Zumbul, Izmir Turkey

I am a world traveler who has read many trip guides but this one really made a difference for me. I would call it a heartfelt creation of a local guide expert instead of just a guide.

-Susy, Isla Holbox, Mexico

New to the area like me, this is a must have!

-Joe, Bloomington, USA

This is a good series that gets down to it when looking for things to do at your destination without having to read a novel for just a few ideas.

-Rachel, Monterey, USA

Good information to have to plan my trip to this destination.

-Pennie Farrell, Mexico

Great ideas for a port day.

-Mary Martin USA

Aptly titled, you won't just be a tourist after reading this book. You'll be greater than a tourist!

-Alan Warner, Grand Rapids, USA

Even though I only have three days to spend in San Miguel in an upcoming visit, I will use the author's suggestions to guide some of my time there. An easy read - with chapters named to guide me in directions I want to go.

-Robert Catapano, USA

Great insights from a local perspective! Useful information and a very good value!

-Sarah, USA

This series provides an in-depth experience through the eyes of a local. Reading these series will help you to travel the city in with confidence and it'll make your journey a unique one.

-Andrew Teoh, Ipoh, Malaysia

GREATER THAN A TOURIST- BIRMINGHAM ALABAMA USA

50 Travel Tips from a Local

Sophie Mace

Cover designed by: Ivana Stamenkovic
Cover Image: https://pixabay.com/photos/birmingham-alabama-city-cities-
1603396/

Image 1:
https://commons.wikimedia.org/wiki/File:16th_Street_Baptist_Church.JPG John
Morse [CC BY-SA (http://creativecommons.org/licenses/by-sa/3.0/)]
Image 2: https://commons.wikimedia.org/wiki/File:Birmingham_Skyline.jpeg
Amcannally [CC BY-SA (https://creativecommons.org/licenses/by-sa/4.0)]
Image 3:
https://commons.wikimedia.org/wiki/File:Railroad_Park,_Birmingham.jpg
Jrbawden [CC BY-SA (https://creativecommons.org/licenses/by-sa/4.0)]
Image 4: https://commons.wikimedia.org/wiki/File:RegionsFieldBham.png
Alabamadem [CC BY-SA (https://creativecommons.org/licenses/by-sa/4.0)]

CZYK Publishing Since 2011.
Greater Than a Tourist

Lock Haven, PA
All rights reserved.

ISBN: 9798612774891

>TOURIST

50 TRAVEL TIPS FROM A LOCAL

BOOK DESCRIPTION

With travel tips and culture in our guidebooks written by a local, it is never too late to visit Birmingham. Greater Than a Tourist- Birmingham, Alabama United States by Sophie Mace offers the inside scoop on The Magic City. Most travel books tell you how to travel like a tourist. Although there is nothing wrong with that, as part of the 'Greater Than a Tourist' series, this book will give you candid travel tips from someone who has lived at your next travel destination. This guide book will not tell you exact addresses or store hours but instead gives you knowledge that you may not find in other smaller print travel books. Experience cultural, culinary delights, and attractions with the guidance of a Local. Slow down and get to know the people with this invaluable guide. By the time you finish this book, you will be eager and prepared to discover new activities at your next travel destination.

Inside this travel guide book you will find:

Visitor information from a Local
Tour ideas and inspiration
Save time with valuable guidebook information

Greater Than a Tourist- A Travel Guidebook with 50 Travel Tips from a Local. Slow down, stay in one place, and get to know the people and culture. By the time you finish this book, you will be eager and prepared to travel to your next destination.

OUR STORY

Traveling is a passion of the Greater than a Tourist book series creator. Lisa studied abroad in college, and for their honeymoon Lisa and her husband toured Europe. During her travels to Malta, an older man tried to give her some advice based on his own experience living on the island since he was a young boy. She was not sure if she should talk to the stranger but was interested in his advice. When traveling to some places she was wary to talk to locals because she was afraid that they weren't being genuine. Through her travels, Lisa learned how much locals had to share with tourists. Lisa created the Greater Than a Tourist book series to help connect people with locals. A topic that locals are very passionate about sharing.

TABLE OF CONTENTS

Play Like The Locals

12. Feed Giraffes At The Birmingham Zoo
13. Stop And Smell The Roses At The Botanical Gardens
14. Get High At High Point Climbing And Fitness
15. Watch The Trains At Railroad Park
16. Become A Scientist At The McWane Center
17. Shop Til You Drop At The Summit

Hit The Food Scene

18. Get The Queso, Cocktails, & Tacos At Rojo
19. One Word: Pizitz
20. Satisfy Your Sweet Tooth At The Birmingham Candy Company
21. Drink A Cocktail With A Killer View
22. Go On A Brewery Hop
23. Try The Secret Sauce At Milo's
24. Get Your Crepe On At Red Cat
25. Order Your Sweet Tea 1/2 & 1/2
26. Drink Coffee With The Purrrfect Companions

Get Your History On

27. See The Site Of The Famous 16th Street Baptist Church Bombing
28. Take The Freedom Walk Through Kelly Ingram Park

Seasonal Events

DEDICATION

This book is dedicated to Mamie for always reminding me "il faut bien profiter de la vie" and for being the best grandma a girl could ever ask for. And to Michael, my favorite travel buddy for life. I never want to stop exploring the world with you. Special thanks to my parents for all the support given to me during this book adventure and to my best friend for always believing in my writing.

ABOUT THE AUTHOR

Although she wasn't born in Alabama, Birmingham has slowly become home for Sophie. She did the latter half of her adolescent years into adulthood growing up in the Magic City where she attended University. She studied journalism where she found her love for writing and her true passion shines throughout her creative writings and blog posts. Sophie created and writes her own blog, TypicalSoph where she shares her traveling adventures and overall lifestyle. Traveling is a huge part of Sophie's life as she believes that immersing yourself into other cultures is the most rewarding and best feeling. Although she frequents Europe because of her native French roots, she hopes to one day be able to capture her own stories in as many countries on as many continents as possible.

Besides writing, Sophie loves to see the world behind her camera lens and loves to share her story through images of past sights she's seen. When she isn't writing or taking photos, Sophie can be found outdoors either at the crag rock climbing or on a trail running or hiking. When she isn't being active, she likes to go to coffee shops or spend time at home with her cat Pistachio.

HOW TO USE THIS BOOK

The *Greater Than a Tourist* book series was written by someone who has lived in an area for over three months. The goal of this book is to help travelers either dream or experience different locations by providing opinions from a local. The author has made suggestions based on their own experiences. Please check before traveling to the area in case the suggested places are unavailable.

Travel Advisories: As a first step in planning any trip abroad, check the Travel Advisories for your intended destination.
https://travel.state.gov/content/travel/en/traveladvisories/traveladvisories.html

FROM THE PUBLISHER

Traveling can be one of the most important parts of a person's life. The anticipation and memories that you have are some of the best. As a publisher of the Greater Than a Tourist, as well as the popular *50 Things to Know* book series, we strive to help you learn about new places, spark your imagination, and inspire you. Wherever you are and whatever you do I wish you safe, fun, and inspiring travel.

Lisa Rusczyk Ed. D.
CZYK Publishing

WELCOME TO
> TOURIST

16th Street Baptist Church, now a National Historic Landmark

Birmingham skyline at night from atop the City Federal Building, July 1, 2015

View of Birmingham from Railroad Park

Regions Field

"The real voyage of discovery consists not in seeking new landscapes, but in having new eyes."

- Marcel Proust

Although originally from North Carolina, Birmingham has now been my home for fourteen years. This upcoming city is home to some seriously cool spots and writing this book has given me a newfound love for my current hometown. From a historically rich story to the ultimate foodie's dream, Birmingham is the whole package. Let's not forget about the outdoor scene for all us outdoor enthusiasts. This is my guide complete with tips for some of my favorite places to visit and things to do that I have found out by exploring in my daily life. I hope you find a little magic in the Magic City like I did.

Birmingham
Alabama, USA

Birmingham
Climate

	High	Low
January	51	33
February	56	37
March	67	44
April	75	51
May	82	60
June	88	68
July	91	72
August	91	71
September	84	65
October	74	53
November	66	46
December	55	36

GreaterThanaTourist.com

Temperatures are in Fahrenheit degrees.
Source: NOAA

THE BIRMINGHAM WAY OF LIFE
1. BIRMINGHAM IS H-O-T!

Y'all Alabama summer heat is no joke. If you plan to visit Birmingham in the summer, then prepare to reach a whole new level combination of heat and humidity. The heat is one thing, but the humidity adds a whole other level to it. I'm talking a sweltering, constantly sweating, can never seem to cool down type of level. Learn to complain about the heat and you'll fit right in. Nah, I'm only slightly kidding. Birmingham is hot, but definitely not unbearable. However, there are a few tips and tricks to help in combating the Alabama heat.

First, drink water, drink water, and drink even more water. When you think you've drunk enough, drink even more. Staying hydrated throughout the day will really help you feel better in this good old Alabama heat and your body will thank you. I like to keep a reusable water bottle with me when I am on the go and with the tap water being safe to drink in Birmingham, I'm never without water.

Second, if you plan to do anything and I mean anything outside, do it at the crack of dawn or when the sun is setting. These can be the only bearable and

17

sometimes safe times to be outside during a very hot day.

Three, bring a jacket everywhere you go. The hotter the temperature outside, the colder the air conditioning. It's just a fact of life. So when you go to sit inside of a restaurant or enter any sort of store, be prepared to be blasted with the AC. Going from the direct heat to the freezing cold will seem nice at first, but you will get cold. Bring a jacket with you, because no matter how many times you ask for your server at a restaurant to turn down the air conditioning, they probably won't do it.

Lastly, just be smart. It isn't uncommon to be under a heat advisory during the Alabama summer months. Check the weather and plan your activities accordingly. Use the heat to your advantage. Getting too hot? Go for some ice cream. After all, you are just trying to cool down, right?

2. SOUTHERNERS LOVE SMALL TALK

Be prepared to make small talk because Southerners love to talk about anything and everything. From getting the latest deal on a sale to the outcome of that week's football games, you're sure to have someone trying to talk to you at any given place. Southern charm really is a thing and everyone in this city is very friendly. We just want someone to complain with about the heat in the summer and cold in the winter, if you can even consider it the cold. Other major topics include how bad traffic is or if you're lucky, how bad it wasn't, the humidity level, and really just football again.

People here have that small-town chat with everyone mentality even though Birmingham is a pretty large and populous city. Not every culture, city, or country is like this, but be prepared to strike up a conversation because everyone wants to talk to everyone here. At the very least "hello" or "how are you?" are guaranteed to be exchanged more often than not. Keep an open mind and make the small talk; it will make some people's day.

3. KNOW THE MEANING OF THE SUSPENDERS

Any Birmingham native or person residing here knows and understands the importance of "the suspenders" of local chief meteorologist James Spann. In simplest terms, if Spann is on your television screen and you can see his suspenders, then things are getting serious. His iconic suspenders have come to signify when bad weather is approaching and with Birmingham weather being very unpredictable this could really happen on any given day, especially during storm season. What started off with Spann just taking off his jacket because he was too hot in the studio has now become his way of getting people's attention. The removal of his jacket into suspender's mode is actually part of his thought process. Jacket on and things are all good. Jacket off with his suspenders showing then he thinks we're in danger. And if he thinks that we are in an absolute emergency, he will roll up his sleeves with his suspenders still present. With severe storms and tornadoes always being a possibility in this state, knowing the meaning of the suspenders is a bit of an Alabama joke, but also kind of important.

4. THE APPROPRIATE RESPONSE TO "WAR EAGLE" IS "WAR EAGLE"

Alabamians take their college football VERY SERIOUSLY and Alabama is home to two major college football teams: the Auburn Tigers and the Alabama Crimson Tide. Birmingham is pretty much the center between the cities of Auburn and Tuscaloosa, which are the homes for these two major teams. Due to the location of Birmingham, you get the mixture of Alabama and Auburn fans which can get a little messy at times. When someone tells you "War Eagle" the appropriate response is "War Eagle", it's kind of Auburn's way of saying "hello" to other fans in a sort of identity and greeting. Similarly, the appropriate response to "Roll Tide" is, you guessed it "Roll Tide". Now if you're caught up in a display of rival banter then you'll hear the responses interchanged meaning an Auburn fan will tell an Alabama fan, "War Eagle" instead of "Roll Tide". Being in Birmingham and hearing these phrases spoken is odd at first, but it happens so often especially around football season that you'll just get used to it.

5. SPEAKING OF FOOTBALL... GAME DAYS!

If you're traveling to Birmingham during prime football season, then you'll be immersed in the hectic of Alabama football. As I mentioned, Alabamians take their college football very seriously. The huge rivalry between the Crimson Tide and the Auburn Tigers makes Birmingham a hub for die-hard fans pledging allegiance to their teams. Of course, as a traveler to Birmingham, you may not know or care about these teams, but game days can still be fun. Taking a day trip down to Tuscaloosa to watch the Crimson Tide play or up to Auburn to watch the Auburn Tigers is a unique and traditional southern way to spend any given Saturday during football season. Even if you do not plan on attending a game, the day trip is still worth the experience. The energy felt in these two cities on game day is pretty unreal. Tailgate before the game and then head to a sports bar to catch the game with thousands of fans. Just remember "War Eagle" for Auburn and "Roll Tide" for Alabama, you do not want to get these mixed up.

Want to stay in Birmingham? Look for any sports bar and you can enjoy the game while eating typical game day foods and craft beers. As long as you stick with a sports bar, you're guaranteed to be watching the game with a bunch of other people so you can still experience that southern football-loving aura. If you want to watch the game on a more low-key level, then you can head to almost any restaurant in Birmingham and they will also be showing it. A good rule of thumb is if the place has a TV, then they are showing the game(s).

If football really is not your thing, then use this time to go do anything without even the slightest of a crowd. Birmingham becomes a bit of a ghost town whenever Auburn and/or Alabama are playing, especially during home games. This is my absolute favorite time to go out into the city and experience places that are otherwise pretty crowded.

6. PLAN YOUR 280 TRIPS ACCORDINGLY

280: It's a number that Birmingham natives have come to loathe and despise, some even shudder when the number is uttered and it all has to do with one highway. Highway 280 is the multi-lane highway in Birmingham. This stretch of road spanning over four lanes, sometimes three, sometimes even just two will connect you to all things great about Birmingham. What's not great? The traffic that you're sure to encounter. Since this is the main way to get from the east side to the west side of the city and is also the easiest way to get to and from other major interstates, you're sure to be with a few hundred other people on this highway at any given time.

The problem with this highway is all of the traffic lights that span the length of it. With everything being located off 280, then traffic lights every quarter mile or so is the necessary evil and the more stoplights present, the more congestion there will be. It's just another fact of life.

Plan your Highway 280 trips accordingly and try not to travel it during any and all hours that could be considered rush hour. If you absolutely have to travel 280 during prime hours, then look for back roads. They will be your best friend and save you ample time, even if it only saves you from traveling a short portion of 280. Let's face it, no one wants to spend their entire day sitting in traffic let alone waste part of your trip. Highway 280 can also be a bit unpredictable, which brings me to my next tip.

GENERAL TIPS

7. BECOME A WAZER

Download the Waze app and use it every time you plan to drive anywhere in Birmingham. As I already mentioned, Highway 280 can be quite unpredictable, but it doesn't end with just that specific highway. The other major interstates that cut through and connect the city of Birmingham can also be just as unpredictable and become congested. If you're driving anywhere during rush hour, then you're guaranteed to hit traffic, after all this is a city where you have to rely on cars to get around. But what if you're driving and it isn't prime traffic time, are you home free? Unfortunately not. I have been living in Birmingham for fourteen years and have still yet to understand the patterns of us Alabamians. You could hit no traffic at all at a certain time on any given day and try to repeat that same drive on another given day, and the two traffic patterns could be as different as night and day.

Download and use the Waze app to cut down on driving time. For those of you who are unfamiliar with Waze, it is a driving app that gives you the best route with help from other drivers in real-time. The app is interactive so you can make your contributions while on a drive to alert others of any road problems such as traffic, accidents, or even police officers. Waze will find you the fastest and most efficient way for you to get from point A to point B, so you can enjoy all of what Birmingham has waiting for you, without wasting unnecessary time. Travel like a local so you can have time to play like a local.

8. SPEAKING OF DRIVING... RENT A CAR

Good old Birmingham, the city that relies on cars to be able to get around. Public transportation practically ceases to exist in this city, so you really should plan on renting a car. With many of the things to experience being so spread out across the city, driving will be the only way to get you there, and you don't want to limit your options by not being able to get places.

There is a bus system, but I would use it only as a last resort because it will take up huge chunks out of your day. Unlike other cities that have perfected the bus system, Birmingham's bus system is limited with many routes not having enough buses scheduled to

run them. Uber is also an option but can get costly.
Renting a car will be the most cost-savvy and
efficient option for you to enjoy everything that
Birmingham has to offer. Plus you'll get to join the "I
hate 280 club." firsthand, making you an honorary
Birmingham-ian.

9. PACK FOR ANYTHING

Seriously pack for any and every weather possible.
Birmingham weather is anything, but predictable. So
whether you're coming for a week, a few days, or
even just one day, you're sure to experience the crazy
Alabama weather. In any given week (or day even),
you can experience four different seasons. It's like
Birmingham flips a coin to decide the weather each
day. It could be freezing cold in the morning just for
it to be really warm in the afternoon or vice versa.
Birmingham also likes to grace us with monsoon-like
rainstorms, flooding the terrain and then still have the
sun come out to say hi that same day. About the only
thing that is predictable weatherwise, is the humidity.
Birmingham almost always has a high humidity rate.

The only tip I can give you to face the
unpredictability that is Birmingham weather is to just

pack for anything. Coming in the Summer? Pack those shorts, t-shirts, and sandals, but also pack your rain gear, jackets, and umbrellas. Coming in the winter? Still pack those shorts, t-shirts, and sandals because it isn't uncommon for the temperatures to be in the 70s, but also pack your winter boots, sweaters, and cold weather attire. Checking the weather in advance really should only be used as a rough guide because the weather can change in the blink of an eye. Come prepared unless you want to purposely come unprepared so that you can have a reason to go shopping. I won't tell anyone.

10. CARRY QUARTERS

Like in any major city, parking in downtown Birmingham can be an absolute nightmare. One thing that is sort of lacking in Birmingham is the presence of public lots and parking garages. There are a few, but they are mainly used for the hospitals and the university located in the city which means you're basically going to be stuck street parking. With street parking comes those lovely quarter eating metal meters. Folks, just pay those meters. It's one of those tedious tasks that we just don't want to do, but the dollar you'll save is not worth the risk of getting a ticket. Depending on the area, the meter maids hand out tickets so fast, I swear they must be wizards of some sort.

If you're parked near the University of Alabama at Birmingham or in 5 Points in Southside then I would say you definitely have to pay the meter. If you're more in the midtown area or center of downtown, then you may be able to get away without paying one. Look for smaller "side" roads which will sometimes have un-metered free two-hour parking or around Railroad Park which has free parking as well.

There are plans to implement a more convenient and digital way of paying for parking with your smartphone in the near future because let's face it, we are in the 21st century and everything has become digitized. However, until that happens, you're at the mercy of the coins.

11. PLACES TO STAY

Staying in the right spot can make or break your trip. Since I'm a local living in Birmingham, I've never had to stay in a hotel or other public accommodation, but I have lived in different areas of the city. So, here is my short guide for where to stay during your trip to the Magic City. First and foremost, I highly recommend staying in the downtown area. This really is where Birmingham comes to life and many of the places I mention in this book can be found downtown. You'll get a real Birmingham local vibe and won't have to spend x-amount of time traveling places.

If you really want to tap into that local feel vibe then opt for an Airbnb, which will let you stay in an apartment or house. This is great for people who prefer a home away from home atmosphere and you can find some really unique looking ones. If you're more of a hotel kind of person, then Birmingham has plenty to choose from including one of a kind boutique hotels and well-known chain hotels.

Looking for that one of a kind stay? The Tutwiler is one of Birmingham's oldest hotels and will provide you with a unique stay in this historic gem. This hotel has since been renovated, but the original marble floor and vaulted ceilings can still be seen today. The hotel is located downtown in a prime location to many restaurants and bars making for a convenient stay. Rumor has it that a ghost resides in this little historic gem and guests have experienced knocking sounds on their doors at night. So if you're into ghost haunts, this one may be for you.

Maybe the ghost thing isn't for you, not to worry, there are other boutique hotels to enjoy like the Elyton Hotel. This hotel is also located in the center of downtown and features modern and elegant decor. Enjoy southern cuisine at their restaurant or head to the roof for a cocktail at the rooftop bar, which you will learn all about later on in this book.

If boutique hotels aren't your thing and you like to plead loyalty to a specific hotel chain, then you will find just about every major hotel chain throughout Birmingham, many of which are located in the downtown area.

PLAY LIKE THE LOCALS

12. FEED GIRAFFES AT THE BIRMINGHAM ZOO

This is easily one of my favorite things to do in Birmingham. I mean who doesn't like getting up close to these magnificent creatures while easily becoming their new best friend? Okay, maybe they just take a liking to you because of the handful of leaves in your hand, but shh we won't tell anyone. You will have to pay a small fee to enter the giraffe feeding encounter, but it is worth it and makes for some amazing photo opportunities and some even more amazing memories. The Birmingham Zoo does an amazing job with this encounter and the animal specialists will tell you all about your new friends.

If feeding giraffes isn't your idea of fun, there are plenty of other things to see and do at this zoo, including daily feedings and animal training, which you can find out all about on the Birmingham Zoo's official website. Not to be missed is their newer exhibit: "Trails of Africa", which features male African elephants, and puts the Zoo as a national leader in the conservation of threatened elephants. This zoo also has an impressive story concerning

Babec, a Western Lowland Gorilla who received the first-ever successful cardiac resynchronization therapy device.

This 122-acre Zoo, which focuses on conservation efforts and education, and features around 700 animals is definitely worth a visit. Make sure to check out their Zoolight Safari event which showcases Christmas light displays and illuminations if you plan to be here during the holiday season.

13. STOP AND SMELL THE ROSES AT THE BOTANICAL GARDENS

Figuratively and literally speaking because the Birmingham Botanical Gardens features an impressive rose garden with roses of every color imaginable. Cut through this rose garden on your way to the other sections of the Gardens for a truly scenic walk. My personal favorite place to visit is the greenhouse, which is located on the right side of the Gardens. Note, this greenhouse is closed on Mondays. Inside you'll be immersed with all sorts of greenery including cacti, banana trees, and even a small waterfall. Directly behind the greenhouse, you'll come across the food garden which is always neat to see. Here you'll find all sorts of vegetables, fruit, and herbs that are grown and then donated to a local food charity. Make sure to check out the lily pond toward the front entrance as well to see the brightly colored water lilies that tend to be present year-round.

Walk further into the Gardens towards the left side and you will find yourself in the Japanese Gardens. Get lost inside the bamboo forest or just enjoy the tranquility of the bonsai garden. No matter what time of the year you plan to visit, the Botanical Gardens is a great way to spend a relaxing few hours and is the perfect spot for a nice leisurely stroll.

Trying to spark some creative juices? The Gardens are the perfect place to do some writing, photography, or just some overall life thinking. The Botanical Gardens is one of my favorite places to get my creativity going and makes for some awesome photography outings. It's really any photographer's, amateur or professional, paradise. Want to take home part of the gardens with you? The Botanical Gardens features a gift shop where you can find the perfect plant to become a new plant parent to. Extra bonus, the Gardens are free to visit. Who doesn't love spending a few hours surrounded by beautiful plants while not having to spend any money?

14. GET HIGH AT HIGH POINT CLIMBING AND FITNESS

High Point Climbing and Fitness is one of two of Birmingham's only climbing gyms and the only one that features rope climbing. Whether you're a climbing newbie, an avid climber, or someone who doesn't even like to climb stairs, there is something here for everyone. It is a great way to spend a few hours or even an entire day as a whole family. Traveling alone? The community at High Point will make you feel right at home and you can definitely find someone to climb with at almost any given time. Check out the kids' room for some serious fun. Whether you're a kid or just one at heart, the kid's room is one of the best rooms at the gym. Who doesn't love climbing "skyscraper buildings" or escaping lava while climbing up a dinosaur wall?

Day passes are good for the entire day and allow you to come and go throughout the day. The gym is located off of Highway 280, which basically means you have all sorts of options for a mid-climb or post-climb snack. Here on a Sunday? High Point offers discounted day passes after five in the afternoon.

The gym features auto-belay routes so if you're not belay certified you can still have a rocking time in the gym. However, if you want to expand your route options and gain some climbing knowledge, then you can also take their basic belay class. I recommend this for anyone who might enjoy climbing even in the slightest. After the class, you can use your new skills to send (the word for climbing a specific route in climber's terms) all sorts of walls. The facility also has a bouldering room if bouldering is more your speed. Still feel the need for a further workout? The gym also offers a weight room, cardio room, and yoga classes, all of which are included with a day pass. There really is something for everyone at High Point.

15. WATCH THE TRAINS AT RAILROAD PARK

Located in the heart of downtown, you'll find a beautiful 19-acre park. Although small in size, this park packs a serious punch. I think my favorite thing about Railroad Park is all the diversity that is present at one time. You can stand in the center of a patch of grass and surrounding you will be all sorts of people, both young and old doing all sorts of activities.

Basically you can name an activity and there is probably someone doing it which means you can feel right at home no matter what you want to do here. You'll even see yogis practicing, people dancing, and hippies playing hacky sack. Railroad Park also has a trail that goes around the entire park and cuts throughout the middle making it perfect to join fellow runners for a run or just go for a leisurely stroll. The park also features an outdoor gym complete with all the equipment needed to prove that you're a fit warrior or if you're like me, just struggle to do one pull up on the pull-up bar.

If you're feeling more of a chill kind of day, then Railroad Park has several patches of grass perfect for a picnic, cloud gazing, or just chilling.

The view from this park is absolutely gorgeous. Being in the center of downtown, you're surrounded by all sorts of buildings, and cutting through the outskirts of the park is a railroad with trains that can be seen passing through on the daily. This adds such a unique character to the park. At one given point, you could see a train rolling through, be among the tall city buildings, and see people playing around in a park. Railroad Park is where urban meets industrial meets typical park greenery, making it a one of a kind place.

While at the park your ears are likely going to be filled with the sweet tune of an ice cream truck. An ice cream truck or two can usually be found on any given day permitting that the weather is nice. Tap into your inner childhood and get a classic Tweety Bird popsicle. You know the one I'm talking about with the gumballs for eyes that just screams nostalgia. If you are not in the mood for ice cream, you can grab all sorts of snacks at the Boxcar Cafe located under the pavilion.

Railroad Park also hosts a variety of events throughout the year that brings the community together. They host so many different events that I don't even know where to begin. If you're in Birmingham during the winter, check out their Brrrmingham ice skating rink. Lace up your skates and enjoy Birmingham's only outdoor ice skating rink. Here during the summer and looking to get active, stay healthy, or just enjoy some entertainment? There are so many events to chose from. The Blue Cross and Blue Shield of Alabama sponsors a "Get Healthy on the Railroad" series which features different exercise classes every weekday from March to October. Whether you're a yogi and want to attend a yoga class or you want to show off your dance moves in a Zumba class, these

39

classes are a fun and great way to get active. Better yet, these classes are all free to attend. There are also free cooking classes on the first Sunday of every month between April and September. Finally, looking for some entertainment? The Alabama Symphony Orchestra puts on a series of free summer concerts. Grab a blanket, bring some snacks, and enjoy the musical sounds of this talented group of people while watching the sunset. The perfect end to a summer day. A full list of events can be found on Railroad Park's official website.

16. BECOME A SCIENTIST AT THE MCWANE CENTER

The McWane Science Center is the spot for all of your educational and science-y needs. This center features four floors of interactive exhibits that will leave you feeling like a scientist. The perfect outing for the family as kids love learning about why and how things work. Do not be fooled though, the adults will have a blast too. Let's not pretend like you aren't curious to find out your reaction time or to lie on a bed of nails.

This museum will have you entertained for hours. Go for the combo admission and catch a film at the IMAX theater that shows a rotation of films on science, nature, and even sometimes movies. The IMAX also features a concession stand so you can have all of your classic movie snacks as you watch a documentary. Do not forget to go to the basement level to see the closest thing that Birmingham has to an aquarium. Although, it isn't an aquarium you can see the exhibit on Alabama's aquatic systems and also touch stingrays and sharks in their touch tank which is pretty neat.

The McWane Center is located downtown and has an attached parking deck and you can pay for your parking when you purchase your admission tickets. Trying to beat the crowd? Go during a weekday as crowds will be at a minimum which makes exploring everything more fun. Leave the McWane Center with more knowledge than when you arrived, unless you're already a scientist.

17. SHOP TIL YOU DROP AT THE SUMMIT

The Summit is probably Birmingham's best and most popular spot for shopping. This outdoor mall is conveniently located off of Highway 280 just past the interstate making it accessible for all travelers alike. Here you'll find something for every array of style and fashion sense imaginable. From home goods and decor stores to clothing boutiques and everything in between, you're sure to find something for everyone on your shopping list, or you know just yourself. If you're a shopaholic then you can definitely make a day out of shopping at the Summit, or just dip in for a store or two while traveling on 280.

Shopping on a weekend? Start early because The Summit tends to get very crowded on Fridays, Saturdays, and Sundays. What can I say? Southerners love their shopping.

If you need a break from lugging around all of those shopping bags head on over to one of the restaurants that The Summit has to offer. Here you'll find everything from chain restaurants to smaller local restaurants to quench that mid-shopping hunger. Pro-tip, plan your eating breaks during off-peak meal eating times. Like I said, The Summit gets very crowded and waiting for a table at a restaurant is just wasted time. Go mid-afternoon for a smoother food outing.

The Summit also features different events like summer concerts and fitness classes like Yoga. These can be found on their official website. If you're here for the holiday season, The Summit puts on a Light Up at the Summit event which is family-friendly and features a Christmas parade, firework show, and the man himself, Santa.

The Summit really is a great spot to go shopping. Besides the many shops and restaurants to choose from, the location of it is beautiful. Located at the top of a hill off the highway, the view if standing at the right spot can be magnificent. To get a look at the city, head on over to the parking garage located behind Chuy's Mexican Food. Situated at the top of this parking garage rests the perfect Summit photo opportunity as well as just a different vantage point of the city facing the east side of 280. Speaking of photo opportunities, check out the "BHM" wall mural next to Trader Joe's and between Barnes & Noble.

HIT THE FOOD SCENE

18. GET THE QUESO, COCKTAILS, & TACOS AT ROJO

I couldn't write a book about Birmingham without including one of my favorite restaurants in this city. Based on the constant crowd though, I'm guessing other people share in my opinion. Rojo is located in Highland Park which is in downtown Birmingham and it serves both American and Latin-Fare food. This aesthetically cute and sort of funky restaurant serves some of the best food and drinks in Birmingham. Order the queso as a starter to lay the foundation for the rest of the delicious food that will follow. As I said, it can get pretty crowded so even though it is a counter service restaurant, there can be a bit of a wait for the main dishes, which are a hundred percent worth the wait. The queso, however, will come out so quickly that it might beat you to your table and you will thank me for having ordered it. My go-to dishes are always from the Latin-fare side of the menu and I have actually never ventured into trying the American side. What can I say? I really like tacos. Given the tasty state of the Latin-fare food, I'm going to go ahead and say that the American-fare won't disappoint either.

The inside of Rojo is a bit on the cozy side, but the decor and style are pretty unique. The best place to sit, however, is outside on the patio under the string lights.

Rojo is more than just a bar/restaurant, they also have an attached event space that hosts a variety of weekly events including live music and sport viewing parties. I love the community feel I get when I eat at Rojo and the business gives back to various local charities by donating a percentage of profits on Tuesday evenings. Did I also mention that they have a brunch menu offered on Saturdays and Sundays with drink specials including Mimosas? This place has a little bit of everything and will remain a favorite among Birmingham.

19. ONE WORD: PIZITZ

The Pizitz Food Hall is essentially a food court with different local food companies and is a must-stop for everyone in Birmingham. Who doesn't love to support small local businesses while enjoying great food? Sort of a two in one. Inside you will find something to satisfy each and every one of your taste buds.

The Pizitz is located in a historic building that used to be a department store and was once considered the heart of downtown. This repurposed building was transformed into what it is today as a way to bring it back to life. Although renovated to be any foodie's dream, the architecture of the building is still really cool and ornate and is worth a visit on its own. There is a parking garage attached to the Pizitz making accessibility easier, which is a plus because as mentioned, downtown parking can be a bit of a nightmare.

Inside the food hall you can find food from all sorts of international cuisine, from Israeli food to Vietnamese to Himalayan specialties, all the way to classic American food. The thing that is so great about the Pizitz is that you can eat one type of food while everyone else in your group eats something completely different, making it the perfect place for groups of people who can't agree on a single place to eat. It also makes a really neat place to try a little bit of everything; from poke bowls and falafel, all the way to candy and waffles, there is something here for everyone. Wash it all down with an alcoholic beverage from The Louis Bar located in the center of the hall, which serves craft cocktails, beer, and wine. Or try an artisan tea from Piper & Leaf.

On the hunt for a unique souvenir? Yellowhammer Print Shop is also located inside the Pizitz. Here you'll find t-shirts with Birmingham specific landmarks, phrases, and designs. If you've ever dreamed about owning an "It's nice to have you in Birmingham" t-shirt, here is your chance. They come in a variety of colors and are super soft. They also have poster prints, home goods, and tote bags.

If you visit on a nice day, step outside and sit on the patio located outside the Piztiz. This is the perfect place to just chill or have a nice friendly, or not so friendly cornhole competition among your friends.

20. SATISFY YOUR SWEET TOOTH AT THE BIRMINGHAM CANDY COMPANY

This hometown candy store can be found inside the Pizitz Food Hall and definitely does not disappoint. Satisfy that sweet tooth of yours and indulge in an assortment of candy and other sweet treats. I don't know how they do it, but The Birmingham Candy Company makes hands down the best caramel I have ever tasted in my life. Their homemade sweet gooey caramel will make your taste buds literally smile. You really can't go wrong with any of their products, but a fan favorite is their pecan paws. These pecan clusters contain caramel goodness and are topped with either milk or dark chocolate. They also have an assortment of caramel apples year-round which is perfect if you're like me and crave a caramel apple the other nine out of twelve months of the year that isn't Fall. Other treats include truffles, fudge, caramel clusters, and depending on the time of the year, s'mores. They also have traditional candy if chocolate isn't your thing.

If you're lucky to go on a day where the two owners are present then this is a treat in itself. This sweet couple is sure to put a smile on your face, if you're not already grinning like a kid in a candy store, literally. Don't overthink it, just hop on down there and sink your teeth in candy heaven. After all, we all deserve to treat ourselves every now and then, or if you're like me a little more often than every now and then.

21. DRINK A COCKTAIL WITH A KILLER VIEW

Did someone say rooftop bar? That's right in the heart of Downtown Birmingham you can find a rooftop bar or two. Who doesn't like standing on the top of a building above the hustle and bustle down below and better yet, with a drink in hand? The Elyton Hotel features its own rooftop bar known as Moon Shine and will allow you to gain a new perspective of Birmingham. Although this boutique hotel is fancy fancy, the bar at the top has a casual dress code which means you can head over there at any time without worrying about what to wear. Don't be fooled though, you'll still feel very fancy drinking atop a building, or at least I always do. Just walk straight into the Elyton Hotel and take an elevator up the seventeen stories until you reach the top, entering alcoholic delight with a killer view. Moon Shine has a full-service bar with its own specialty cocktails as well as a selection of wine and beer. The drinks can be a bit pricey, but the view is priceless.

Feeling hungry? They also serve small plates and wood-fired oven creations including pizza. The best part is that no reservations are required so you are welcome anytime which further offers that welcoming feel. If you're trying to avoid the crowds, then go early during the afternoon for a day drink. Can't decide on whether you want to see the city during the day or during the night? Get the best of both worlds and go right before sunset. That way you can see the view during the day, watch the sunset while sipping on a drink, and then see the nighttime view of the twinkling city lights down below.

The bar features two separate outside seating portions, the main one and one hidden in the back. Check out the back section as it offers a different vantage point than the main patio. Outside you'll find plenty of comfy seating, heat lamps if you choose to visit during the winter and endless photo opportunities. Don't let bad weather deter you from experiencing this bar. I've been on a particularly windy day and spent the majority of the evening getting blasted in the face by the wind. It's all part of the memories and Moon Shine's bar is located indoors where you can seek shelter from the wind, rain, or that good old Alabama heat. Moon Shine rooftop bar really is a nice place to relax, have a drink or two, and enjoy the view. The perfect stop to begin or end your night or for a day drink.

22. GO ON A BREWERY HOP

Birmingham is definitely not short of breweries, so if you're into the beer scene, going on a brewery hop around the Magic City will be the perfect way to spend a day. You can visit and tour different breweries or just chill around the brewery trying all the craft beers your heart could desire. Starting off with Alabama's oldest and largest brewery, Good People Brewing Company. This brewery is located right across the street from Railroad Park as well as Regions field where Birmingham's baseball team plays. This makes it a great location for visiting before or after catching a baseball game. It was the first brewery to open in Birmingham and a must-try is their Good People Muchacho Mexican lager. You can tour their taproom on Saturdays if you want to see where the magic happens.

Moving on to another large brewery is the Cahaba Brewing Company. This brewery offers tours of their taproom and tasting room. Inside the tasting room, you can sample beers from unique small batches and beers that are not even available outside of the taproom. Their must-try is the Cahaba Blonde which is an American blonde ale that is popular among the locals in Birmingham.

Up next is TrimTab Brewing which was voted in the "top ten under-the-radar craft breweries to watch for in Spring of 2019" by Forbes. This brewery has a pretty neat story behind its name and it all surrounds a ship's trim tab and how it applies to each and every one of us. Learn about the history behind the name while you try one of their double IPAs or sours. What's really cool about this brewery is that their tasting gallery actually doubles as an art gallery for local artists to showcase their work.

Other breweries include, Back Forty which has a kitchen within their brewery serving pub foods, Ghost Train which houses a small distillery within their facilities, and Avondale which is located in a historically rich building that once housed a saloon, firehouse, and post office. Avondale Brewery also has The Sour Room which focuses on sour beers.

As I said, the beer scene is huge within Birmingham. Only you can visit and try the craft beers to decide which one is your favorite.

23. TRY THE SECRET SAUCE AT MILO'S

We all love a good fast food restaurant…the crispy fries dunked in ketchup, juicy burger, and cold refreshing soda. What if I told you that Alabama has its own fast-food chain? Milo's is a fast-food restaurant specializing in hamburgers and is known for its secret hamburger sauce. Established by a Mr. Milo Carlton back in 1946, this chain has evolved to over twenty locations that can only be found in Alabama, mostly in Birmingham. Their original Milo's Hamburgers are topped with pickles, onions, and then soaked with their famous secret sauce making it a unique and distinct taste from the classic American burger. Not a fan of burgers? Dunk those fries in the secret burger sauce, because who says only burger lovers get to try the secret sauce.

Another thing Milo's is famous for is their sweet tea and it is a true Alabama staple. You can find Milos sweet tea bottled on the shelf in just about any grocery store, after all it is the South and we love our sweet tea. Whether you are a fan of the secret sauce-covered burgers or just a fan of the crispy fries like me, your stomach will leave full and happy. After all, there's a reason that "Everybody goes to… Milo's".

24. GET YOUR CREPE ON AT RED CAT

If you're like me and crave a crepe on a good weekend morning, then you have to try The Red Cat. This coffee house is my favorite place to get coffee in Birmingham and one of my favorite ways to start off a Sunday morning. The Red Cat at Railroad Park has a special menu featuring both sweet and savory crepes on Sunday mornings until noon. I, being a complete sucker for Nutella filled crepes, always opt for the Italian one, which features a healthy, or not so healthy, serving of Nutella, bananas, and rice crisps. Feeling something more on the savory side? The Dutch is a bacon, Gouda cheese, and tomato filled crepe. If you don't crave crepes as this girl with French roots does, the Red Cat also has their everyday breakfast and lunch menu as well as baked goods. The best part, they serve their everyday breakfast menu all day which means you can still catch all those z's sleeping in and still have breakfast. I mean who says breakfast has to start before noon?

Now that we got the food stuff out of the way lets talk coffee after all this is a coffee house. The Red Cat has a nice variety of handcrafted coffees and their menu is super clever and on point with the theme.

Their signature lattes are named after different cat breeds. Will you go for a Bengal? Sip on a Russian Blue? Maybe you're more of a Persian. Either way, you can never go wrong. My go-to is the "Bengal", which features dark chocolate and caramel. These come both hot or iced, or if you're feeling adventurous you can get it blended. If drinking cat breed lattes doesn't sound appealing to you, they also serve classic coffee shop drinks as well as hot teas.

Food and drink, check, now let's talk location. The Red Cat Coffee House is located across the street from Railroad Park which makes it perfect to hit up both places one after the other. My go-to weekend morning routine is to go to this cafe, enjoy some breakfast, and then hop across the street to take a stroll through Railroad Park while finishing up my daily latte. Due to the prime location of this coffee shop, it can get pretty crowded especially since it is a little on the cozy side. If you want to try to beat the crowd, head on over to their original and bigger location over in Pepper Place also located downtown. Note, the original location, however, gets very crowded on Saturday mornings due to the farmer's market. Other than that, this location is very chill and unique. Whether you choose the more lively Railroad Park location or the chiller Pepper Place location, The

Red Cat is the perfect spot to stop, drink a coffee, and have some breakfast.

25. ORDER YOUR SWEET TEA 1/2 & 1/2

You're in Birmingham, soaking up the southern heat and want to drink the standard beverage of the South, however you get more than you bargained for. Sweet tea is a staple, but be prepared to receive actual sweet tea when you order sweet tea. I'm talking sugary liquid that will make your face pucker upon swallowing what essentially is cups of sugar with a splash of tea. Order the sweet tea, but order it 1/2 & 1/2 unless you have an insane tolerance for overly sweet things. I have both watched other people in the restaurant industry and have physically had to make sweet tea myself, so trust me when I say that a crazy amount of sugar gets added into that tea urn. Half unsweetened tea and half sweet tea will still give you all of the delicious taste of that sweet southern drink just at an actual drinkable and enjoyable state. The added bonus, you can indulge in dessert after cutting your sugar intake in half. It's all about the balance, right?

26. DRINK COFFEE WITH THE PURRRFECT COMPANIONS

Birmingham now has its very own one and only cat cafe located in Avondale. Gatos and Beans is the spot if you want to play, hang out, and make new furry friends. Although advertised as a coffee shop, the true star of the show is the cat room. You can get coffee anywhere, but Gatos and Beans is the only place you can go chill with cats who are actually only living there temporarily. This coffee shop is partnered with a local animal rescue group and all of the cats that are at the cafe are up for adoption. So you may not only leave fully caffeinated but also with a new cat companion.

You have to pay an entrance fee which includes a standard coffee or soda and then you are free to hang out in the cat room for an hour. It kind of makes for an expensive coffee drink, but the way I see it, it's like you are donating or contributing to a cat shelter. It's not exactly the same, but all of these cats are temporarily living there until they find their forever home. Plus, can you really put a price on getting to spend time with cats?

I'd recommend going to Gatos and Beans during the week as they tend to get booked up on the weekends, especially on Saturdays. They take reservations and recommend making them, but like I said if you go during a weekday as opposed to a weekend then you should be fine without one.

The owner is really nice to chat with and you can tell that she is very passionate about all of the cats that reside there. If you go on an off-peak day, then be prepared to have a conversation with her, as I mentioned we love to make small talk in the South.

My favorite thing about this cafe is getting to see all of the different cat's personalities. Some will keep to themselves while others will hop into your lap for a cuddle. The worst part is having to part with your new furry friends that you made. Last time I went, I had to wake up a sleeping cat who had taken my purse hostage as their new bed. If you're a cat lover like me, then saying goodbye to these cats can be a painful goodbye, but knowing they're well taken care of and will eventually find their forever home softens the blow. Definitely check this cat cafe out for a fun and different kind of cafe outing.

GET YOUR HISTORY ON

27. SEE THE SITE OF THE FAMOUS 16TH STREET BAPTIST CHURCH BOMBING

Birmingham is home to the very famous site of the tragic loss that provided a pivotal turning point in the United States for the Civil Rights Movement. On 16th Street you can see the church where the famous Ku Klux Klan (KKK) bombing took place back in 1963, killing four young girls. This church was the first African-American church in Birmingham and became a meeting point for civil rights leaders such as Martin Luther King Jr and Fred Shuttlesworth. The church was a location for organizing and educating marches.

On the morning of September 15th, 1963, members of the white supremacist group the KKK planted fifteen sticks of dynamite under the steps of the church. The bombing killed four girls and injured more than twenty other individuals. This tragic bombing became a monumental point in history and was the first of its kind. Bombings had been present prior, causing the nickname of "bombingham" to be used. However, the church bombing was the first that caused lives to be taken and provided support for passing the Civil Rights Act of 1964.

The church is still an active church today and you can visit the inside of it. Here you can see the memorial for the four children, whose lives were taken, where the bombs went off. Inside the church, you can also see a stained glass window that was donated by the people of Wales in memory of the girls.

This sobering and humbling site is worth visiting while in the city that is pretty much synonymous with the Civil Rights Movement. This church is part of the Civil Rights Trail and this as well as the Kelly Ingram Park and the Civil Rights Institute will provide you an insight into this crucial part in America's history.

28. TAKE THE FREEDOM WALK THROUGH KELLY INGRAM PARK

The next stop as part of the Civil Rights Trail is the Kelly Ingram Park. This park is located in the Birmingham Civil Right District and is directly outside the famous 16th Street Baptist Church. This four-acre park was the site for many Civil Rights

Movement demonstrations making it a historically rich location to visit.

While walking throughout this park, you will come across different statues and sculptures related to the Civil Rights Movement. These powerful statues depict the struggles in the city which Dr. Martin Luther King Jr. coined as "the most segregated city in the United States". Among these statues are commemorative sculptures of MLK, Fred Shuttlesworth, and other heroes of the Civil Rights Movement.

You will also come across vivid depictions of police brutality, assaults, and the use of police dogs on marchers and demonstrators. These sculptures are eye-opening and harrowing but should be on anyone's list when visiting Birmingham. You can experience the history of key events during this important era in U.S. history by taking a walk through the park's "Freedom Walk".

Another impressive sculpture you will find at this park is the Four Spirits sculpture which was created in memory of the four girls who died in the 16th Street Baptist Church bombing. This statue shows the four girls getting ready for the church sermon on the morning of the bombing which is what they were doing in the basement of the church when the bombing happened. If you look closely at the sculpture you can actually see the photographs and names of two teenage boys in addition to the four girls. These two boys were also killed on the day of the bombing when they were both shot.

What's really cool about this park is that you can actually take an audio tour with the use of your cell phone. During this audio tour, you will be guided through the significance of each of the sculptures. You can access the tour by calling a free number that can be found online.

29. LEARN ABOUT THE CIVIL RIGHTS AT THE CIVIL RIGHTS INSTITUTE

The last stop for the Birmingham portion of the Civil Rights Trail is the Birmingham Civil Rights Institute. This large premier museum depicts the struggles of the Civil Rights Movement and aims to "enlighten each generation about civil and human rights by exploring our common past". This museum tells the story of the past in "a positive way to shape a new direction for the future". The Birmingham Civil Rights Institute is located next to both Kelly Ingram

Park and the 16th Street Baptist Church making it ideal to hit up all three of these in one day.

The museum is closed on Mondays and free to visit on Sundays with donations being asked for. There is a small parking lot located behind the Institute or look for street parking across and then walk directly through Kelly Ingram Park.

Inside the museum, you will find exhibits showcasing Birmingham's role during this era and the human rights struggles that were faced. Listen to the voices of the participants who took part in the Civil Rights Movement through a multimedia exhibit called the Oral History Project. Films and displays throughout the museum can also be found and will enlighten you as it embodies the history of African-American life during their struggle for civil rights.

Displays of how things, businesses, and schools were segregated give you an eye-opening look for what it would've been like growing up during that time period. You will also learn about the 16th Street Baptist Church bombing and the roles of key heroes during the Civil Rights Movement.

This Institute is an important stop to your Birmingham trip and I recommend visiting all three stops on the Civil Rights Trail to learn about our city's history and a point in history that was so crucial for the United States.

30. TAKE A SELF-GUIDED TOUR THROUGH THE FURNACES

An iconic attraction for visitors to Birmingham is Sloss Furnaces. This tour will give you a different kind of experience compared to everything else to see and do because it really is one of its kind for the city. Sloss Furnaces is a National Historic Landmark that will provide you with an industrial look into the place where the "magic" in the Magic City began. Today it still stands as it did when it was in use for eighty-eight years becoming the longest continually ran furnace in the city's history.

You will pass by the Furnaces if you drive through the downtown area, but don't let that be your only view of it. The Furnaces are free to visit and you can take a self-guided tour to learn all about the history behind the process and products created by these furnaces. Self-guided tour means you can spend as little or as long as you'd like at this Industrial Revolution monument. They will provide you with all of the reading materials to help you become a pro on the history of the Furnaces that built Birmingham. If you prefer to take a guided tour, then those are offered on the weekends.

The industrial vibe and outright history of Sloss Furnaces makes it the perfect backdrop for all sorts of photography. If you're an amateur photographer like myself, then you are free to photograph and practice your skill without paying a fee. However, if you have tapped into the professional photographer world then you must register and pay to be able to use these furnaces as your muse.

Of course, the Furnaces no longer have iron flowing throughout them. However, it is still used for metal arts that are poured there to keep the history alive so to speak. Workshops are offered for welding and blacksmithing, but the main type of art they create at the Furnaces is cast iron art. So if you ever wanted to try your hand at casting, here is your chance.

Sloss Furnaces also hosts a concert venue which is unique in its own sense. If you're into catching a concert, check out the events because you may luck out and be visiting Birmingham during one.

31. GET SPACEY AT THE SPACE CENTER

Birmingham is pretty central when it comes to the geography of Alabama which makes it the perfect place to be able to take day trips from. One of those day trips that I recommend making is to the "Rocket City" also known as Huntsville, Alabama. Hop in your car and take the short one and a half-hour drive to this city. Although there is so much you can see and do in Huntsville, I would say the must-see thing is the U.S. Space & Rocket Center. Whether you're really into space exploration or would rather leave that to the professionals, this Space Center is a must-stop for everyone. This space museum is the largest of its kind in the World. That alone should be enough to make it on the top of your list. Here you can learn all about the history of space exploration in the exact city that is responsible for developing the rockets that put man on the moon.

I won't lie, I am not really big on the subject of space in general, but I had a great time when I visited this space center. There are so many impressive and neat things to see inside from permanent and traveling exhibits to simulations and even a planetarium. Seeing all sorts of artifacts from the US space program was really neat and was a bit eye-opening and surreal to see. It's crazy to see how people live and travel for space exploration.

The World's only full-scale fully stacked transportation system also known as a space shuttle can be seen in Shuttle Park at the center while Rocket Park has different rockets used throughout history. My favorite part, apart from the ride simulations because I'm a total sucker for any amusement type ride, is definitely the Saturn V Hall at the Davidson Center (still part of the US. Space & Rocket Center). Inside this hall, you can see one of only three Saturn V rockets on display in the world. Now, the whole center is impressive, but this Saturn V rocket is out of this world, no pun intended. You will feel like you've shrunk in size when you stand under this rocket and this hall alone is worth the drive to Huntsville.

This center is so big with so many things to see and do that you could actually spend multiple days visiting the Space Center. The museum seems more like an amusement park and without a map, you could quite easily get lost. Some of the exhibits are in different buildings while some are outside. There are also space travel simulators in the form of rides that are fun and included with the admission price. Fun for the kids and adults alike. This includes a space shot that simulates a rocket launch, a G Force Accelerator where you can experience three times the force of gravity, and a HyperShip motion-based simulator that provides a multi-sensory experience centered on different movie-like presentations. You can leave feeling like a real astronaut after conquering all of these simulators.

Now, I know I just said that my favorite thing was the Saturn Hall, but another big favorite of mine is the planetarium. Although not included with the price of admission, I think the planetarium is worth splurging for. This planetarium offers an 8K digital dome experience and uses 5 state of the art Christie laser projectors synchronized. Do I know what that means? Absolutely not. Do I know that the Planetarium is worth the visit? Absolutely! The shows they offer are both entertaining and educational. I watched one where we traveled into the solar system and took a look at all of the planets and I was thoroughly upset when it ended. The show featured an actor who was acting out along with the show being projected which was a unique touch. The only problem with this planetarium is trying to decide which show you'll choose to watch, but my guess is you can't really go wrong with any of them.

Astronaut training, check. Rockets viewed, check. Planetarium show watched, check. Now it's time for the gift shop because of course, no space center trip would be complete without a trip to the gift shop. Here you will find so many different space-themed items because like everything else at the space center, this gift shop is huge. From t-shirts and toys to pins and patches, you will struggle to decide what to buy. What really stood out for me were these toy doll girls that were dressed in astronauts as part of a girl in STEM line and I almost bought one of these for myself. The gift shop has a lot of cool things and if you ever wanted to try freeze-dried ice cream or other astronaut freeze-dried food, now is your chance. Learn about space exploration, train and eat like an astronaut, and leave feeling like an astronaut after you visit The U.S Space & Rocket Center

32. CLIMB THE ICONIC STATUE

The most iconic attraction to see in Birmingham is the Vulcan Park & Museum. This unique statue of the Roman god of fire and forge stands for our city's iron origins and is the world's largest cast-iron statue.

71

Situated at the top of Red Mountain and towering at fifty-six feet tall, Vulcan watches over the city providing you with hands down the best view in the city. You can climb to the top of the statue to the observation deck, where you'll get a 360-degree view. The front of the statue faces downtown Birmingham with his spear pointing upwards while his backside faces the suburb of Homewood, iconically becoming a joke as he moons the city with his butt naked backside. A song was even created to pay homage to the fact that Vulcan has been mooning Homewood for decades.

Both the museum and the observation deck at the top of Vulcan are included with daily admission as well as entrance to the park grounds. If you want to see Vulcan after the nightfall, the statue itself and the park grounds are open for visiting, however, the museum is not. The Visitor's Bureau of Birmingham also operates an official information center at this park and museum which makes it the perfect stop for visitors to learn more about what Birmingham has to offer.

The statue was created by a sculptor named Giuseppe Moretti and it was presented at the St. Louis World's Fair to highlight Birmingham and the city's growing industrial abilities. There is a great deal of history surrounding the statue and how it became the exact one that stands over Birmingham today and you can find out all about it at this interactive history museum of Vulcan. Here you can learn everything about Vulcan and Birmingham's story, as well as see past pieces of the statue like the traffic safety torch that was removed after being present for over fifty years.

Vulcan has become such an idol for the entire city of Birmingham that you will see both his name and his image used all over the place as advertising strategies for businesses. The image and his name are so symbolic, that they are both registered with the U.S. patent trademark office.

Outside the official grounds of the park and museum, you can find a public two-mile running/walking trail open from dawn to dusk. Found at the bottom of the front side of the statue, the trailhead features its own parking lot and is home to the future hub for a planned seven hundred and fifty mile Red Rock Trail System. I recommend checking this spot out as the first mile of the trail provides a scenic view of the city skyline throughout varying tree clearings. Pro-tip, go around sunset for a vibrant and picturesque view.

OUTDOOR TRIPS

33. CLIFF JUMP AT HIPPIE HOLE

Little River Canyon is home to one of Alabama's greatest swimming holes: Hippie Hole. This is another day trip I recommend making if you're visiting during the hot months and are looking for a unique addition to your vacation. Here, you'll swim with the locals at a popular spot while soaking up that country river vibe.

Little River Canyon is located in the northeast of Alabama, about an hour and forty-minute drive from Birmingham. If you're looking for a scenic way to spend the day then a trip to this National Preserve in the Southern Appalachians is the way to go. Although there is so much to Little River Canyon, Hippie Hole is the place to go if you only have a day to experience it.

Free to visit with free parking at the trailhead, Hippie Hole can be accessed through a short albeit steep hike down to the falls. You'll definitely want to bring a cooler in with some snacks as your stomach will get that peckish feeling from swimming. I know that I am not the only person who gets really hungry after being in the water for a while. Pack that cooler with snacks as well as drinks to re-hydrate because the Alabama sun is no joke, but like I said be aware that the hike in is a little steep and you will have to carry it all down to the falls. The more you bring, the harder the hike, but the better the day you'll have. Note, alcohol is not permitted and they sometimes have park rangers checking inside your coolers.

Speaking of things to bring, don't forget to wear outdoor sandals with straps so you don't lose them in the water or even better, water shoes. The rocks in the river can be both sharp and slippery. Your feet will appreciate the protection. If you're planning to cliff jump and swim in the actual swimming hole then I recommend bringing a float or pool noddle with you. Even if you're a strong swimmer, having one of these to float around with can be a game-changer. Lastly, don't forget a towel. This may seem like an obvious, but can easily be forgotten. Not only will you want it to dry off with but the rock surfaces on the sides of the river and swimming hole heat up in that hot sun and having a towel to sit on will save you from getting burned.

As I mentioned there is cliff jumping. Get your adrenaline rush by jumping off from one of three different cliffs at varying heights. The water in the swimming hole is deep enough but watch for rocky areas when jumping. Watch how the locals do it and follow suit and you'll be fine. Not into the cliff jumping? Gathering around the swimming hole and watching people cliff jump is a fun activity in itself. It's also pretty cool to see people build up the courage to jump off the very top one. Speaking from experience, it's a scary jump, but worth it for the adrenaline rush.

Hippie Hole also has a river that flows with shallower pockets for wading making it the perfect spot to cool down if you don't want to swim in the swimming hole. Hippie Hole is the summer spot for Alabama natives and we don't mind sharing; just keep Alabama beautiful and carry out any and all trash you bring in with you.

34. PLAY IN THE CAHABA

Playing in the Cahaba is like a rite of passage for all Birmingham natives. This river is the largest river in Alabama and is one of the most biologically diverse rivers in America and it just so happens to run through Birmingham. The Cahaba river runs one hundred and ninety-four miles and empties into the

Alabama River. This scenic waterway can be accessed in many parts throughout the city leaving you with a few different options for taping into that Birmingham way of life.

My absolute favorite way to experience this river is by paddling down it via kayak or canoe. Depending on where you access and how far you go this can be a trip that takes a couple of hours or one that can take an entire day or even days. Assuming you won't be traveling with your own gear, you can rent a kayak or canoe through a company called "Canoe the Cahaba".

Another way to experience this scenic river is by tubing. Limestone tubing located in Brierfield, Alabama just outside of Birmingham provides you with everything you need for a unique trip down the river. Limestone tubing actually takes place on the part of the river known as the Little Cahaba. The company provides you with both the inner tubes and shuttle trips, making it just so you have to show up and float down the Cahaba. Bring a cooler with drinks and snacks, and stick it in its own inner tube to make the leisurely trip beside you. Wear water shoes or shoes you don't mind getting wet because the trip down can get rocky at times especially if the water level is on the lower side.

Another option for experiencing the Cahaba is simply by swimming. If you choose to do this, watch for the water quality that is monitored by the Cahaba River Society. Check for water levels and weather patterns to ensure safety. A popular spot for swimming is a swimming hole along the Grants Mill Road or in the Little Cahaba off of Highway 280. For a complete guide to swimming the Cahaba, you can find the Swim Guide online.

35. TAKE THE ICONIC KING'S CHAIR PHOTO

Alabama's largest state park is located in Birmingham's very own backyard and I personally feel very fortunate for it. At 9,940 acres, Oak Mountain State Park is home to one of the widest variety of outdoor activities of any state park. The problem comes with trying to decide what to see and do during your one day visit, although the park does offer both cabin and backcountry camping if one day doesn't seem like enough, which it really isn't.

If you can see and do only one thing while at Oak Mountain, I suggest making the hike up to the King's Chair Overlook and taking the iconic King's Chair photo. This hike follows the blue trail off of the North Trailhead and features a pretty hefty two-mile incline to the top. Make sure you bring fuel to re-hydrate especially if you choose to make the hike in the summer heat. The great thing about this hike is that when you reach the top the views become that much more rewarding after the moderately strenuous hike up. The overlook features a small seat made out of the rocks hence the name King's Chair. Sit in this chair and take the iconic photo. The views from up there are stunning and will leave you breathless. No, not from the hike up, I'm talking the view itself will leave you with that breathless feeling.

If you aren't feeling up to the hike up to King's Chair, another great and popular hike is to Peavine Falls. Peavine Falls is located off of the South Trailhead and although a bit steep on the way out of the Falls, it is a much shorter hike. The best time to visit the Falls is after plenty of rainfall, leaving a good amount of water flow in the Falls. Note- if it hasn't rained in a while, the water will be very low and it isn't uncommon for it to be a mere trickle. Recent rainfall or not, the drive up to the Peavine Falls trailhead offers a scenic drive up a windy and uphill road. You can park towards the top before reaching the trailhead and actually reach an overlook without having to hike. This overlook along the road is my go-to spot to stop and have a nice picnic.

Finally, if hiking isn't your cup of tea, then do not let that deter you from visiting this State Park. As I mentioned, there is a wide variety of other outdoor activities you can experience. The park features a marina where you can rent different types of boats like kayaks and pedal boats. Next to the marina, there is a beach where you can swim in one of the lakes within the park. Other activities include horseback riding, archery, and a pump track for biking to name a few. A full list of activities can be found on their official website.

The park is open every day and you will have to pay a per person entrance fee, but the fee is worth it for a day of outdoor adventures. There are two entrances to the park, the main gate and back gate. If you plan to stop at the North Trailhead then take the back gate to save you from a long drive throughout the park. The last tip, if you plan to hike download the Google maps for the park. Although all the trails are nicely marked, the park features over 50 miles of trails leaving many of them to intertwine. Having the map in your pocket with you will save you from turning your supposed two-mile hike into a six-mile hike, trust me this happens.

36. GET AN ADRENALINE RUSH

Red Mountain Park is another large outdoor park that you should consider visiting while in Birmingham. This 1,500-acre park is home to one of the most historically significant new park projects in the United States, and Birmingham's rich history can be seen throughout the park. Red Mountain was the site for iron ore mining in the past and remains of these mines can be found throughout the hiking trails making it a one of kind park in Birmingham.

Get your adrenaline pumping and book one of the many different kinds of adventure trips at Red Mountain Park. I recommend doing the Vulcan Materials Zip Trip. This trip features seven different zip lines, a sky bridge, and a rope swing. Children will love it and so will the adults. I'm an adult and I had a blast when I did my adventure trip. You will get your adrenaline rush going while you tap into that inner child again while climbing among the trees. There is something nostalgic about climbing, swinging, and playing around outside and Red Mountain allows you to experience that feeling. Other activity trips include their mega zip line which will have you soaring through the trees for 1,000 feet and their one of a kind adventure tower. Make sure you book these adventures beforehand because space is limited.

When you're finished playing like a kid again during your adventure outing, don't go home just yet. Red Mountain Park has many other things to see like two different outlooks over the city and rope bridges to be explored. My favorite hike to make is up to Grace's Gap Overlook, one of the two overlooks to experience at this park and in my opinion the better of the two. There are many ways to get to this overlook depending on how long of a hike you want to make, but it will be at least a two-mile hike to reach this destination. At the overlook, you will see a view of Birmingham's skyline from a distance. You will also come across the Rushing Rendezvous treehouse. Attached to this treehouse is the biggest suspended bridge in the park. This hike is great to make because you get a two in one with the overlook and the treehouse.

Red Mountain Park is great for families and people of all ages. The hiking trails, treehouses, and urbex vibe spewing from the mine remains are what make this park different from others. Download the trail map before setting off on your hike and as always, take out anything you bring in. This park is free to visit, but a suggested donation of three dollars is asked to help with the continued development of the park.

Oh and one last thing, if you're traveling with a pup, check out the dog park. Remy's Dog Park is a popular spot among the locals and their furry friends. The dog park is a short hike in towards the front of the park.

THINGS TO SEE

37. WATCH THE SUN SET OVER THE CITY

Birmingham has some amazing, photo-worthy sunsets. It's like Monet himself glides his paintbrush of colors painting the entire city of Birmingham a beautiful sunset every night. Golden hour is hands down one of the prettiest times to be outside or by a window in Birmingham. The best part is that the sun always seems to come say goodnight even after a big storm. Now, of course, you can see the sunset pretty much anywhere throughout the city, but the best place to view it is on the Red Mountain Expressway. This road connects the city of Homewood with downtown Birmingham and does so by passing above the city near Vulcan. Park your car at the Vulcan trailhead right off this road and walk alongside the Red Mountain Expressway towards the city view until you're in the clearing of the trees. Take camp at this spot and watch the beautiful colors painted in the sky above the city skyline. This really is an incredible view and probably my favorite in all of Birmingham. Snap some photos or just stand in the moment; either way, enjoy.

38. SEE COLOR AT THE COLOR TUNNEL

The color tunnels are arguably Birmingham's most popular photo-worthy spot and you really can't go to the Magic City without experiencing the tunnels. Yep, you read that right, there are actually four separate color tunnels to experience. Meaning you're sure to get the perfect shot after your color tunnel adventures. The original tunnel is located on 18th street under the railroad underpass. This art installation was created by Bill FitzGibbon as a way to transform these dark and deemed scary underpasses that connect the north and south sides of Birmingham. These underpasses were widely underused at the time, but with their rainbow lights, they now draw people. This permanent light installation uses LED lights that can change colors and speed. Besides the original 18th street location, the other three tunnels can be found under the viaducts at 14th, 19th, and 20th streets. The tunnels are obviously better seen at night as the colors are a lot more vibrant against the contrast of the dark sky. The tunnels feature sidewalks making it pedestrian-friendly. Safety concern is expressed surrounding the topic of the color tunnels, but I personally have never felt unsafe walking through any of the tunnels. Note that homeless people may reside under these tunnels, but they are not panhandlers and most likely will not bother you. You can always drive through the tunnels as well which makes for a cool experience during your commute between the north and south sides of downtown. Whether you walk through or drive, definitely give one or all four of these tunnels a visit.

39. LEAVE YOUR MARK ON THE MORRIS AVENUE MURAL

"Before I Die I want to _____" is the prompt, the answers are an endless possibility that only you can decide. Under the 21st Street bridge on Morris Avenue, this public engagement mural exists prompting you to think and reflect on life while making it the perfect place to leave your mark in Birmingham. Express yourself to others with what you want to experience or achieve in life and receive a new outlook and perspective while you read other people's desires. Some are humbling and will make you smile, some will even make you laugh. Others may open your eyes to finding inspiration for bucket list items you may never have thought of. Either way you look at it, this chalk covered wall is worth a visit.

40. SPEAKING OF WALL MURALS...

Wall murals are a creative way to add color, messages, and art to different parts of the city that would otherwise blend in with the other building infrastructures and Birmingham is home to some really cool looking ones. Checking out different wall murals is like going to an enlarged art museum spread out over the city. If you see only one while you're in Birmingham then definitely check out the classic "It's Nice to Have You in Birmingham" located off of Richard Arrington Jr. Boulevard downtown. This classic mural is a must-stop photo opportunity for every Birmingham traveler, whether you're a first time visitor or an Alabama native.

There are wall murals located all over the different cities within Birmingham so you're not limited to seeing these works of art in just downtown. One of my favorites is actually on the side of a coffee shop in the city of Hoover. This piece painted on the side of Santos Coffee Shop features a quetzal bird with its wings spread out. Over and behind the bird is a sunset with a silhouette of the Birmingham skyline complete with Vulcan. The quetzal bird is the national bird of Guatemala and Santos Coffee features signature coffee from Guatemala so this beautiful mural isn't just pretty to look at, but also stands as a symbol for the business. That's the great thing about all the murals across Birmingham, they aren't just pieces of art. Although really impressive to look at some are there to convey messages and meanings, promote businesses, and honor history. As you've come to know, Birmingham is rich in its history and one mural in particular honors the 50th anniversary of the Civil Rights Act. This can be found downtown on 18th Street South on the side of a Wells Fargo bank.

Another really great one to see is the Birmingham color wall located on 1st Avenue North. This is also one of my favorites to go look at because it stands for so much more than just the initial color-infused wall your eyes first see. This mural came together as part of a public event where around 600 people turned up to. Although colorful and vibrant, the wall wasn't just created by another artist, it was created by the people of Birmingham, which I find unique and adds a whole other alluring element to it. Wall murals really do

89

brighten up and make the city unique in its own way and Birmingham is home to so many that you could really make a day out of exploring them.

41. WALK THE COBBLESTONE ROAD

A cute cobblestone road from the past that can be a little tricky to find at first, but is worth the hassle of driving around in circles to find. Stepping onto Morris Avenue is like stepping into an entirely different city. I always get a sort of older traditional city vibe that really just spews historic Birmingham. It's rich in history as most of Birmingham is and is actually on the National Register of Historic Places. This district was once a major spot for warehouses, then transformed into an entertainment and shopping district. Today it is a mix-use spot featuring entertainment, shopping, and lofts. The character of this charming avenue is still very much present, making it a unique spot to explore.

Park your car on one of the adjacent streets because parking on Morris Avenue is very limited and only accessible in one direction. Be sure to bring a camera because the architecture and cobblestone road will make you want to snap all the photos. A few different wall murals can also be found while standing on Morris Avenue, including a huge robot and the "Before I Die" mural.

This avenue has been home to a peanut depot for over a hundred years. Alabama Peanut Company has now acquired the space, but peanuts are still boiled here every day. Step inside and enjoy different kinds of peanuts and see the impressive boiler machines. This place is really a must-stop on Morris Avenue.

Another must-stop is a hidden-away speakeasy that can be found in an alleyway near Founder's Stations, which is now a loft building. This speakeasy named Pilcrow is a bar specializing in agave spirits that pays homage to the printing press that used to reside at the Founder's Station. Pilcrow, being the typographical character for a paragraph symbol was chosen in honor of the history of the building. This low key cocktail cellar is sort of Renaissance meets literature with its unconventional interior decor and is one of my favorite places to go to on Morris Avenue.

Other places to check out include a local restaurant featuring New American fare, a chocolate and clothing store that shares a storefront, and a pub featuring a rooftop bar.

42. FIND OUT WHAT'S ON SECOND

What's On Second is a Birmingham hometown antique store which is actually located on 1st Avenue instead of 2nd. Checking out antique stores is always a fun adventure because you never know what you're really going to find. That mystery element just adds to all of the fun that goes into antique shopping. What's On Second is worth checking out, even if you don't plan on purchasing anything. Old toy collectibles, vinyl records, and antique home decor are all things you'll come across and so much more. It's actually really amazing all of the different things that you will find. This location is a smaller store than their original location as they decided to downsize, but don't worry your eyes will still struggle to see everything packed into this quirky store. I'm pretty sure the last time I went I even saw some locks of hair. Not sure who it belonged to, but locks of hair are there if you want them.

My absolute favorite thing to check out at What's On Second is all of the really old, unique, and just classic photographs and postcards. They have old-timey photographs from all over the world and it's really incredible to see. They also have a collection of

Alabama photographs and postcards which I always tend to forget about, but make an awesome souvenir or collectible in general. Obviously I can't tell you everything that lives inside this store, so you'll just have to go find out for yourself what's on second.

SEASONAL EVENTS

43. MOSS ROCK FESTIVAL

If you happen to be in Birmingham at the beginning of November, then the Moss Rock Festival is a must-see. Located at the Moss Rock Preserve in Hoover, this two-day festival is perfect for lovers of all things art and eco-friendly. Inside the festival, you'll experience art, nature exhibitors, and eco ideas for smart living.

Traveling with kids? This festival is great for little ones and has kid-friendly activities like a climbing wall, rope bridge through the trees, and hula hooping. Okay, that last one is actually for the adults too! They also have a variety of eco arts and crafts for kids to create, like actual paint on boxes and create art with recyclable type art. It's fun, educational, and great for the environment. While the kids have their fun creating art and out hula hooping adults, guests 21 and older can head over to the beer garden where you can sample over sixty craft beers from local Alabama and non-local breweries. The beer garden will cost an additional fee from your entrance ticket to enter, but inside you can sample all the beer you want, enjoy some snacks, and even take home a featured commemorative beer glass. Note, because of state law you will have to pay an additional one cent per beer sample inside the beer garden.

Beer garden and kids corner aside, let's talk about what the rest of the festival has to offer. Artist Row exhibits over a hundred artist tents showcasing and selling their nature-inspired art. Whether you're just an admirer of art or looking for a new cool art piece to take home, Artist Row is always fun to leisurely check out. After walking down the Artist Row, you will come across the SmartLIVING Market. This is basically a farmer's market within the festival itself. Here you'll find fresh and locally made products and food. Anything from soap and candles to cookies and baked goods can be found here. Businesses that focus on healthy body and mind living through the enjoyment of the great outdoors are also showcased here. Live music can also be heard throughout the duration of the festival from local groups and artists that perform on stage in the center of it all.

Built-up an appetite from walking around and looking at cool eco-inspired art? Head on over to all of the yummy food trucks and booths located by the stage. Satisfy your hunger while listening to music, it's perfect.

Due to the secluded and serene location of the Moss Rock Festival, the organization provides free shuttles to and from your car away from it all with parking at the Hoover Met. This works out well and makes parking not even the slightest bit of concern all while keeping the atmosphere of the festival. You can purchase entry tickets in advance online or at the gate. When you're ready to leave, hop on a shuttle back to your car or continue your nature-themed day by going for a hike at Moss Rock Preserve.

44. TRAVEL TO GREECE

Unfortunately, there is no secret tunnel to connect you from Birmingham to the actual country of Greece. However, the Greek Community of Birmingham puts on a really great and what I would say authentic weekend during their Greek Festival which is pretty much the next best thing. This food festival is one of my favorite weekends here in

Birmingham and will transport you into a world of culture, even if only for a few hours. Organized and hosted by the Holy Trinity-Holy Cross Greek Orthodox Cathedral of Birmingham which is the fourth oldest Greek Orthodox parish in the Southeast, it is one of Birmingham's oldest cultural events. This beautiful church opens its doors for self-guided tours throughout the festival and is definitely worth a tour even if just to admire the building itself.

The festival offers delicious authentic food for a great value and donates proceeds to local and national charities as well which is always a plus in my eyes. The festival itself is free to attend as well as the parking for the event. With an entrance fee eliminated, you can spend those extra dollars that you saved on all of the Greek food instead. If you're a dessert gal like me, then definitely try the baklava. This baklava is the real deal and will leave you longing for more. In fact, do yourself a favor and go ahead and buy some to take with you as well.

Speaking of taking food-to-go, the festival even offers a drive-thru feature which means you can try the gyros, dolmathes, pitas, and more without having to even step out of your car. The perfect option for anyone who is in a time crunch. However, the true way to experience this festival is by taking your time and enjoying everything it has to offer. Once you've made the tough decision on what to eat, find a table by the stage and enjoy the entertainment featuring Greek music and traditional Greek dances. Popular items due tend to run out by the third day, so plan to attend during one of the first two days.

As mentioned above, don't forget to check out the dessert room to try the baklava, Greek wedding cookie, or any of their other pastries. The dessert room is separate from the rest of the food area making it more organized for getting dessert after your meal, or if you're like me, dessert first. There is also a Greek Market Place to check out that has Mediterranean foods and Orthodox Christian souvenirs so you can tell everyone you actually "went" to Greece. This festival brings together over 30,000 people each year and you should be one of them. Eat some delicious Greek food, absorb the energy from the authentic entertainment, and leave with a happy and full stomach all while experiencing a culture that celebrates life.

45. WATCH VULCAN LIGHT UP THE SKY

Thunder on the Mountain is Birmingham's very own Independence Day tradition. Watch this amazing firework display shot off from the god of fire himself, Vulcan. This firework show lights up the sky with hundreds of exploding shells and the assortment in the collection of fireworks offers a variety of different color bursts and reports. The firework show can be seen from all over the city, rule of thumb, if you can see Vulcan from where you're standing then you'll be able to see the exploding fireworks behind him. However, the truly best place to see them is up close and center. I'm talking as close to the statue as they will let you get. I love viewing the fireworks from here because not only are you really close to the fireworks and have a direct line of sight, but you also have a fantastic view of the Vulcan statue which is really what makes this firework show truly unique. It's the only firework show shot off from Vulcan and the bursting fireworks make a neat and temporary backdrop for the glowing statue of Birmingham's mascot.

Arrive early before the roads become closed or you won't be able to even hike up the hill to the base of Vulcan. Bring a towel or something to sit on and stake out the perfect viewing spot on the grassy area below the statue and on top of the Red Mountain Expressway. Be prepared for the loud bangs of the fireworks around you. Yeah, firework shows are always loud, but this one resonates with an echo with each and every firework report. There's a reason why it's called "The Thunder on the Mountain". The show is also choreographed to a playlist that can be heard on the Vulcan radio station. This show is one thing Birmingham definitely does right.

46. QUENCH YOUR THIRST ON THIRSTY THURSDAYS

Thirsty Thursdays is a weekly event that takes place at Regions Field during baseball season. The Birmingham Barons is the minor league baseball team that plays in the Southern League and is based in the Magic City. Their home field is located in the middle of downtown, making a sport meets urban vibe. No matter where you're sitting in this field, you will get a lovely view of the city as a backdrop. This American past time favorite is a must-see if you've never been to a baseball game before. Attend Thirsty

Thursday for baseball and beer drinking for the ultimate American duo. As I mentioned, Birmingham has a huge beer scene and we love our craft beers. Enjoy a night of inexpensively priced beers during Thirsty Thursdays. Adults can enjoy drinking while the kids will love playing around the kids' zone that is open for every game.

If beer drinking isn't your thing, then attend a game on a Friday night instead for their Firework Fridays. This firework show goes off after the game, making it the perfect end to a baseball filled night.

The Birmingham Barons has other season-long promotions and theme weeks which you can keep up with on the Barons' official social media handles. Whether you quench your thirst on Thursday or watch the firework show on a Friday, the Barons' games are the perfect spring and summer pastime.

47. HONOR OUR VETERANS

Birmingham is home to America's first and therefore oldest Veterans Day Parade. If you happen to be in Birmingham on Veterans Day you really do not want to miss this historical parade. A World War II veteran and Birmingham native named Raymond

Weeks is actually the reason why we have a national holiday today, known as Veterans Day. He is also the one who led the first National Veterans Day Parade in Alabama back in 1947. Today it is an event you really should see if given the chance.

The parade route circles downtown around the Midtown area and Railroad Park giving you plenty of options to find a great spot along the route. I personally love to view the parade towards the beginning of the route in Midtown just because I like the initial energy and let's face it, I'm impatient.

Make sure you block off at least two hours to view this parade because it is that large. If you plan to capture the parade through a camera lens, make sure you watch the sun patterns because the sun will shift before the parade is over. From veterans to marching bands, to just patriotic people and horses, this parade is something to see. What's really neat is that each of the groups holds up banners that recognize different battles and wars complete with the dates these took place. So not only are these battles being honored, but you get a sense of a timeline for when these things happened. Seeing the older Veterans smiling and waving in the parade is worth seeing in itself and always melts my heart.

48. GET SCARED AT ATROX FACTORY

Birmingham is home to Alabama's largest indoor haunted house and it is a popular attraction among the locals. This quarter-mile haunted attraction is the best and scariest haunted house I have ever experienced. I might be the world's biggest baby when it comes to haunted houses and scary movies, and yet something about Atrox Factory keeps me going back each season. Speaking of season, it is, of course, only open for the Halloween season so you will only luck out with getting to experience this place if you're visiting Birmingham during the fall. The props, scenes, and characters are so well created that it becomes very real very quickly. Is a monster going to really cut you in half with a chainsaw? No. But does it seem like it's going to happen? Yes. The attraction is well-thought-out and executed. The monsters inside the attraction are allowed to touch and grab you, so be prepared to be touched, stroked, and grabbed, especially if you're the most scared one in your group. They pry on us scaredy cats.

The haunted house can only accommodate a certain amount of people each night and they have been known to sell out before closing time on prime nights. Prime nights include Friday and Saturday nights which are naturally busier because it is a weekend but also because they have featured guest stars from popular horror movies on these nights. This is a cool touch if you're into the horror movie scene because this could be your chance to meet a favorite celebrity of yours. However, if you do not care about meeting horror movie stars then skip Atrox on these nights. Not only does it get insanely crowded, but there is also an extra cover charge just to enter the premises. I personally choose to go on weekday nights because it is less crowded and you will not have to wait around nearly as long. Make sure to bring cash with you because the tickets are cash only.

Will Atrox leave you screaming? Yes. Will you be scared? Yes. Will you be glad when you finally escaped? Definitely yes. Give Atrox Factory a visit if you dare.

49. DOG WATCH AT PEPPER PLACE MARKET

Okay, there's actually more to this place than just dog watching. Pepper Place Market is a farmer's market located in the Pepper Place district in downtown Birmingham. It is definitely a pet-friendly event and the perfect place to socialize your dog or just have people ogle over how cute your furry friend is. With outdoor markets running the majority of the year, every Saturday from mid-April to mid-December, this market is a popular spot among the locals. Pepper Place Market was established in 2000 as a way to help local farmers and has grown to include all sorts of Alabama based vendors. Here you'll find fresh produce from local farmers, fresh bread and pastries from local bakeries, and all sorts of craft foods.

Food, however, isn't the only thing you will find at this market; you can also find craft candles and soaps, decor, and lots more. A list of the weekly vendors can be found on the Pepper Place Market website or social media handles. The market takes place rain or shine and is guaranteed to be crowded. Arrive at the crack of dawn to avoid the crowds and have the first pick of everything. Not an early riser?

The market stays pretty well stocked throughout the duration and becomes very lively throughout the morning.

Various food trucks make their appearance each week making it the perfect spot for a quick morning snack. There is even a food truck with purely dog treats. I told you the market was very pet-friendly. Live music can be heard on two different ends of the market and cooking demonstrations from local chefs can also be seen. This market is the perfect way to start off your Saturday. Shop local, eat local, and bring home a local and unique souvenir.

50. EXPERIENCE BIRMINGHAM'S DINING SCENE DURING RESTAURANT WEEK

Restaurant week which is actually longer than a week, ten days to be exact, is an event put on that allows you to try the different cuisines of the city. Participating restaurants feature a special menu or fixed course meal usually at less expensive pricing than normal. In other words, not only can you try delicious food, but you can also eat knowing you're getting a good deal. Some restaurants take part in breakfast, others take part in lunch and/or dinner, but there are so many participating that you could eat out every meal during the week (or ten days) and never have to repeat dishes.

No advanced tickets are required. Just show up and eat out as normal, though some restaurants will take reservations. The restaurants participating change each year with some taking part every year and others being new. What started off with only thirty restaurants taking part, has now doubled making this "Birmingham's premier dining event".

The food scene in the Magic City is growing and Birmingham is one of "the best fifty foodie towns in America" according to Daily Meal. This event taking place in August is the perfect opportunity to really delve into the food creations of chefs in the city. You can find all the information on participating restaurants online as well as what special menu they will be offering making it easier for you to decide which places to go to beforehand, although the many dish options will still make it hard in choosing. Give this event a go, if you happen to be in Birmingham in August and your stomach will leave happy.

BONUS TIP :
PICTURES TO TAKE

As I mentioned, I love to capture the world around me with a camera lens and Birmingham has so many great photo opportunities. Although I touched on a few of them throughout this book, I want to share with you a couple other places to get the best photos during your trip to this city.

First, The Alabama Theatre. This Theatre is located in the Theatre District on Third Avenue North and hosts the perfect backdrop for photos. The flashing "Alabama" sign will transport you to a retro theatre feel. Stand under the sign to get a beautiful memento of your trip to Birmingham.

Another one of my favorite spots to take photos at is on top of the Richard Arrington Jr. Blvd bridge that goes over the railroad tracks. This one-way bridge overlooks the railroad and is a pretty place to take city vibe photos. This is a popular spot for photography shoots in Birmingham.

Lastly, the Rotary Trail, which can be found near Railroad Park. This Trail features a forty-six foot tall sign that says "Rotary Trail in the Magic City" which makes for some cool looking photos. Head over here after nightfall to take photos with the illuminated sign for the ultimate Magic City photo.

TOP REASONS TO BOOK THIS TRIP

1.   **Food**- Birmingham's food scene is really booming with local food spots taking over the city and it is home to some unique cuisine. Your taste buds will be happy after having eaten in one of America's "most exciting food cities" by Zagat.

2.   **History**- The historically rich past of Birmingham is how the Magic City got its name. There was a sense of "magic" in the past where the city just boomed out of nowhere. Come explore what makes this city, The Magic City.

3.   **Outdoor Scene**- Birmingham is situated at the foothills of the Appalachian Mountains, making it the perfect outdoor scene for any and all outdoor lovers. You can experience the city life and then travel out of downtown and be immersed in the great outdoors. Swim in the rivers or hike one of the many trails Birmingham has to offer.

PACKING AND PLANNING TIPS

A Week before Leaving

- Arrange for someone to take care of pets and water plants.

- Email and Print important Documents.

- Get Visa and vaccines if needed.

- Check for travel warnings.

- Stop mail and newspaper.

- Notify Credit Card companies where you are going.

- Passports and photo identification is up to date.

- Pay bills.

- Copy important items and download travel Apps.

- Start collecting small bills for tips.

- Have post office hold mail while you are away.

- Check weather for the week.

- Car inspected, oil is changed, and tires have the correct pressure.

- Check airline luggage restrictions.

- Download Apps needed for your trip.

Right Before Leaving

- Contact bank and credit cards to tell them your location.

- Clean out refrigerator.

- Empty garbage cans.

- Lock windows.

- Make sure you have the proper identification with you.

- Bring cash for tips.

- Remember travel documents.

- Lock door behind you.

- Remember wallet.

- Unplug items in house and pack chargers.

- Change your thermostat settings.

- Charge electronics, and prepare camera memory cards.

READ OTHER
GREATER THAN A TOURIST
BOOKS

> TOURIST

Follow us on Instagram for beautiful travel images:
http://Instagram.com/GreaterThanATourist

Follow *Greater Than a Tourist* on Amazon.
>Tourist Podcast
>T Website
>T Youtube
>T Facebook
>T Goodreads
>T Amazon
>T Mailing List
>T Pinterest
>T Instagram
>T Twitter
>T SoundCloud
>T LinkedIn
>T Map

> TOURIST

At *Greater Than a Tourist*, we love to share travel tips with you. How did we do? What guidance do you have for how we can give you better advice for your next trip? Please send your feedback to GreaterThanaTourist@gmail.com as we continue to improve the series. We appreciate your constructive feedback. Thank you.

METRIC CONVERSIONS

TEMPERATURE

110° F —   — 40° C
100° F —
90° F —   — 30° C
80° F —
70° F —   — 20° C
60° F —
50° F —   — 10° C
40° F —
32° F —   — 0° C
20° F —
10° F —   — -10° C
0° F —
                — -18° C
-10° F —
-20° F —   — -30° C

To convert F to C:

Subtract 32, and then multiply by 5/9 or .5555.

To Convert C to F:

Multiply by 1.8 and then add 32.

32F = 0C

LIQUID VOLUME

To Convert:...................Multiply by
U.S. Gallons to Liters................ 3.8
U.S. Liters to Gallons 26
Imperial Gallons to U.S. Gallons 1.2
Imperial Gallons to Liters....... 4.55
Liters to Imperial Gallons 22
1 Liter = .26 U.S. Gallon
1 U.S. Gallon = 3.8 Liters

DISTANCE

To convert ....Multiply by
Inches to Centimeters 2.54
Centimeters to Inches 39
Feet to Meters...................... .3
Meters to Feet 3.28
Yards to Meters 91
Meters to Yards 1.09
Miles to Kilometers 1.61
Kilometers to Miles............ .62
1 Mile = 1.6 km
1 km = .62 Miles

WEIGHT

1 Ounce = .28 Grams
1 Pound = .4555 Kilograms
1 Gram = .04 Ounce
1 Kilogram = 2.2 Pounds

TRAVEL QUESTIONS

- Do you bring presents home to family or friends after a vacation?

- Do you get motion sick?

- Do you have a favorite billboard?

- Do you know what to do if there is a flat tire?

- Do you like a sun roof open?

- Do you like to eat in the car?

- Do you like to wear sun glasses in the car?

- Do you like toppings on your ice cream?

- Do you use public bathrooms?

- Did you bring a cell phone and does it have power?

- Do you have a form of identification with you?

- Have you ever been pulled over by a cop?

- Have you ever given money to a stranger on a road trip?

- Have you ever taken a road trip with animals?

- Have you ever gone on a vacation alone?

- Have you ever run out of gas?

- If you could move to any place in the world, where would it be?

- If you could travel anywhere in the world, where would you travel?

- If you could travel in any vehicle, which one would it be?

- If you had three things to wish for from a magic genie, what would they be?

- If you have a driver's license, how many times did it take you to pass the test?

- What are you the most afraid of on vacation?

- What do you want to get away from the most when you are on vacation?

- What foods smell bad to you?

- What item do you bring on ever trip with you away from home?

- What makes you sleepy?

- What song would you love to hear on the radio when you're cruising on the highway?

- What travel job would you want the least?

- What will you miss most while you are away from home?

- What is something you always wanted to try?

- What is the best road side attraction that you ever saw?

- What is the farthest distance you ever biked?

- What is the farthest distance you ever walked?

- What is the weirdest thing you needed to buy while on vacation?

- What is your favorite candy?

- What is your favorite color car?

- What is your favorite family vacation?

- What is your favorite food?

- What is your favorite gas station drink or food?

- What is your favorite license plate design?

- What is your favorite restaurant?

- What is your favorite smell?

- What is your favorite song?

- What is your favorite sound that nature makes?

- What is your favorite thing to bring home from a vacation?

- What is your favorite vacation with friends?

- What is your favorite way to relax?

- Where is the farthest place you ever traveled in a car?

- Where is the farthest place you ever went North, South, East and West?

- Where is your favorite place in the world?

- Who is your favorite singer?

- Who taught you how to drive?

- Who will you miss the most while you are away?

- Who if the first person you will contact when you get to your destination?

- Who brought you on your first vacation?

- Who likes to travel the most in your life?

- Would you rather be hot or cold?

- Would you rather drive above, below, or at the speed limited?

- Would you rather drive on a highway or a back road?

- Would you rather go on a train or a boat?

- Would you rather go to the beach or the woods?

TRAVEL BUCKET LIST

1.

2.

3.

4.

5.

6.

7.

8.

9.

10.

NOTES

Printed in Great Britain
by Amazon